See the green seed.

A sweet, sweet bee . . .

gave it to me.

I need to plant . . .

the green seed.

I need to see . . .

what it will be.

I will feed the seed . . .

to see it grow.

Is the seed a weed . . .

or a treat to eat?

Is it a tree . . .

the bee gave me?

Tree, wheat, or weed . . .

peach, bean, or pea.

What will the
green seed be?